BEFORE THE TRANSFORMATION

"God Positioned me to help position you"

By: Ernaysia Woods

Copyright © 2025 Ernaysia Woods

All rights reserved. No part of this book may be reproduced in any form without written permission from the author.

ISBN: 979-8-9989930-2-2
Published by Ernaysia Woods

First Edition
Disclaimer: The views expressed in this book are those of the author and do not necessarily reflect the views of any organizations mentioned.

Dedication

To my beloved great-grandmother, Daisy Mae Woods:

From the time I was just three months old until I turned twenty-two, you held me close and raised me with endless love. You were more than a caregiver—you were my heart, my safe place, and my guiding star.

You always called me your "Black Beauty," and with that love you gave me confidence and purpose. You taught me to stand tall when life tried to break me and to trust and be myself no matter how dark the road seemed.

I will never forget the way you cared for your plants—watering them daily, speaking life into them, and watching them grow. In those moments, you showed me what it truly means to nurture, to give, and to pour into something until it blooms. That same love and patience you showed your plants, you gave to me. You taught me that when we care for others, we don't just help them grow—we also grow ourselves.

Though you went home to be with the Lord on May 3rd, 2017, your spirit still lives in me. Every lesson, every prayer, and every ounce of love you poured into me has become part of who I am. This book is not only my story but also a reflection of the legacy you left behind—the legacy of love, faith, strength, and resilience.

Thank you for showing me how to love deeply, how to care patiently, and how to shine boldly. Your memory inspires me every day to rise, to nurture others, and to carry forward the light you placed inside of me.

I love you, Ma. Love, your Black Beauty.

Acknowledgments

First and foremost, I want to express my deepest gratitude to God, whose grace and love have been my guiding light throughout this journey. It's through His strength that I've discovered my true power and learned to lean into His unwavering support. Writing this book has been a labor of love and a profound journey of self-discovery that reshaped my understanding of purpose.

To my amazing sons—Akeeim Carroll Jr. (my guardian angel), Zy'mere Carroll, Marcus Jr., and May'jour. You are my heart, my purpose, and my inspiration. Your love and encouragement give me the strength to rise each day with renewed energy and determination. Always remember, your belief in me is what keeps me going, no matter what challenges we face. I strive to be the best for you, and I carry you with me in everything I do.

To Marcus Sr. Thank you for always being there when I need you most. Your unwavering support has been my rock through every challenge. You love me deeply, encourage me without hesitation, and remind me of my strength and worth, especially on the days I forget. I'm beyond grateful for you, and I appreciate you more than you will ever know.

To my mentors, friends, and family, thank you for nurturing my growth and teaching me invaluable lessons about resilience, transformation, perseverance, and purpose. Your wisdom has shaped my path and inspired me to empower others.

As I reflect on the incredible individuals who have influenced my life, I'm reminded that transformation is a collective journey. Each of you has left a mark on my heart, and with deep gratitude, I acknowledge your impact. Now, let's embark on a deeper exploration of the true importance of transformation and empowerment in our lives.

TABLE OF CONTENTS

Introduction: Empowerment and Transformation 1

Welcome to Your Journey of Transformation 5

Chapter One: Daily Affirmations 6

Chapter Two: Childhood (Egg Stage) 10

Chapter Three: Grief and Loss..17

Chapter Four: Relocated (Caterpillar Roams) 23

Chapter Five: Marriage (Unravled).. 28

Chapter Six: Family/Friends/Community..............................36

Chapter Seven: Cocoon (Transformation Begins) 42

Chapter Eight: Lessons Learned 47

Chapter Nine: Butterfly (Takeoff) 53

As I Fly 57

The Transformative 5: Daily Steps to a Better You 58

Ten Powerful, Transformative Scriptures.................................59

About the Author..60

Reflective Writing 62

Before The Transformation

By: Ernaysia Woods

INTRODUCTION

Empowerment and Transformation

> "Transformation begins the moment you stop fearing who you'll become."

> **"In order to grow, you must shed your old self and emerge into what lies ahead."**
> — *Ernaysia Woods*

Transformation doesn't happen by accident—it begins with awareness, deepens with willingness, and comes to life through obedience. The quote above? It came from the soil of my becoming. I wrote it from a place of surrender, healing, and breakthrough. And now, I extend it to you.

This book is more than an inspirational activation. It's your permission slip to confront the things you've avoided, to release what no longer serves you, and to rise into the version of yourself that God has already seen.

Growth isn't just about saying goodbye to the past—it's about stepping forward with intention, courage, and faith. You have a powerful force within you: the ability to shift, to grow, and to heal. You're not too far gone. You're not too broken. And you are most definitely not alone.

Empowerment isn't just about overcoming what's around you; it's about recognizing the power already within you. It's about choosing to heal, to grow, and to rise, even when it hurts. As we walk through this journey together, you'll witness the process—the breakdowns and breakthroughs, the pruning and the planting, the stretching and the strengthening.

You'll be challenged to face your flaws, confront your fears, and surrender what you can't control. But most importantly, you'll be invited to keep God at the center—allowing His Word to guide your heart, shape your steps, and anchor your progress.

Let this be your reminder:

Your transformation isn't just a hope, it's your journey. Embrace it with open arms and become the person you were always meant to be.

You control your progress.

And now… It's time to begin

Reflect: What fear do you need to release in order to step fully into purpose?

_____
_____
_____
_____
_____
_____
_____
_____
_____
_____

WELCOME TO YOUR JOURNEY OF TRANSFORMATION

You're not here by accident; something in you is ready. Ready to confront what's been holding you back. Are you prepared to unlock what's been buried within? Ready to rise.

This journey of empowerment is where reflection meets action, and obedience meets breakthroughs. This is where the chains begin to break, and the truth starts speaking louder than your fears.

Throughout these pages, you'll walk beside me—not just as a reader, but as a witness. You'll feel the raw, unfiltered process of transformation: the tears, prayers, faith, war, and healing. Every story, every insight, and every strategy is rooted in my testimony. I didn't just write this. I lived it.

Empowerment isn't just about taking back control—it's about surrendering to the One who already has the plan. It's about facing your flaws with faith, walking in your truth with boldness, and finally seeing yourself the way God has always seen you: capable, chosen, and called.

Let this be your permission to stop surviving and start transforming. To stop shrinking and start showing up. To stop doubting and start declaring:

"I am no longer who I was. I am becoming who I was born to be."

But don't take this journey alone. Invite God in—at every page, every pause, every revelation. His voice will guide you. His Word will anchor you. His Spirit will carry you.

Are you ready to confront what's been hidden, release what's been heavy, and embrace what's been holy all along?

Let's dive in together.

CHAPTER ONE

Daily Affirmations

"The words you speak shape the world you live in."

In this journey of transformation, affirmations are powerful tools that can reshape your mindset and reinforce your belief in yourself. These affirmations serve as reminders of your strength, resilience, and boundless potential. Each one is designed to uplift you, help you embrace your unique journey, and inspire you to pursue your dreams with confidence.

As you read through these affirmations, take a moment to pause and reflect on each statement. Allow the words to resonate within you, filling you with motivation and clarity. Repeat them daily, integrating them into your life as a way to cultivate positivity and foster growth.

Remember, you are the architect of your own reality. With every affirmation, you're building a foundation of empowerment and self-love that will carry you through every challenge and triumph. Let these words be your guide as you embark on this transformative journey.

1. I am a masterpiece, uniquely created with a divine purpose.
2. I am unstoppable; my potential knows no limits.
3. I am worthy of all the blessings that come my way.
4. I am filled with the courage to chase my dreams.
5. I am a beacon of light, inspiring others with my faith.

6. I am resilient; every challenge strengthens my spirit.
7. I am deserving of love and respect from myself and others.
8. I am aligned with my highest self and my divine calling.
9. I am transforming my pain into purpose and power.
10. I am equipped to overcome any obstacle in my path.
11. I am a warrior, ready to fight for my dreams.
12. I am guided by God's wisdom in every decision I make.
13. I am a source of hope and strength for those around me.
14. I am open to receiving abundance in all areas of my life.
15. I am thriving in my relationships, nurturing those I love.
16. I am creating the life I desire, one step at a time.
17. I am anchored in peace, no matter the storm around me.
18. I am overflowing with joy, gratitude, and positivity.
19. I am a testament to God's grace and transformative power.
20. I am the author of my own story, and I choose to write it boldly.

As you embrace these affirmations, remember that each one is a powerful step toward your transformation. Take a moment to write down five affirmations that resonate with you or that you want to start saying to support your journey.

"You are the author of your own transformation. Embrace your journey with unwavering faith and determination, for every step you take is a testament to your incredible strength and resilience."

Reflect: Which affirmations do you need to speak over your life daily starting now?

_____
_____
_____
_____
_____
_____
_____
_____
_____
_____
_____
_____
_____
_____
_____
_____
_____
_____
_____
_____

CHAPTER TWO

Childhood (Egg Stage)

"Even in brokenness, a foundation was forming."

Growing up in Brooklyn, New York, came with layers—some loud and unforgettable, some silent and painful. My story begins before I could even form words.

I was told that my mother gave birth to me just one month after losing her own mother, Barbara Ann. That kind of grief—pregnant and motherless—must have weighed heavy on her. Before I was born, she had an abortion, and her mother told her, "You're not going to have another abortion—you're going to have this baby." That baby was me.

As I've gotten older, I've come to realize that even my existence was a fight. I was kept. I was chosen. And now, knowing that, it makes sense of my purpose. I wasn't just born—I was **declared** into this world.

But shortly after my birth, everything shifted. As I was told, my father's mother came and took me from my mother just weeks or months after I was born. At only three months old, I was placed on a couch in my great-grandmother Daisy's house—and that's where my journey began.

Daisy became my anchor. My protector. My constant. But the house was far from peaceful.

We lived at 285 Clifton Place in the heart of Bed-Stuy, Brooklyn (Nostrand Ave). A small two-bedroom apartment filled with me, my two younger cousins, uncles, an aunt, my great-grandmother, and my father's mother. It was loud, tight, and chaotic. I didn't want for material things, but I *ached* for understanding. I wanted to know why my parents weren't there. I longed for connection—to my mother, to my father, and to the siblings I barely knew.

From about age 3 to 14, my father was incarcerated. He'd write me letters, and I'd read them with respect—because what else could I do? His side of the family was raising me. I had to carry a sense of loyalty even when I didn't feel emotionally safe.

My mother would come around sometimes, but not consistently. I was told she struggled with a mental illness—that she wasn't mentally stable enough to raise me. I didn't fully understand what that meant as a child, but I could feel it. Her presence was unpredictable, and her energy often left me with more questions than answers. Even in the moments when I did see her, there was a distance between us that I couldn't close. I wanted to be close. I wanted to be hers. But something was always off. And as I grew older, I started to piece things together in silence—quietly wondering why she couldn't be what other mothers were to their daughters.

I had questions I was too afraid to ask out loud. Why can't I be with my mom? What's wrong with her? It wasn't until I turned 12 that those questions began forming in my spirit. Before then, I lived in a kind of freedom, kept in the dark. But pre-teen awareness has a way of peeling back the layers.

As an adult, I now understand that her absence wasn't always intentional—it was an illness I didn't have the language for as a child. Till this day, my mother is in a mental institution. My father and I speak often now—we're not as close as I'd like us to be, but I've learned to accept what he's able to give and meet him where he is. As for his mother, the woman who once took me from my mom—after moving from New York and finding God, our relationship has become more forgiving and better. The same goes for my uncles and aunt. I've learned to accept their love for what it is, without expectations, and stay true to the woman I've grown to be.

I later learned I had siblings. My sister is five years younger than me, and my brother is ten years younger. They were being raised by my grandfather. I only saw them on birthdays or random occasions, and as I grew older, their absence began to feel like rejection. *How can someone be related to you and still feel like a stranger?*

It wasn't until I turned sixteen that I began seeing them more often, and slowly, we started to form a sense of bond. But truthfully, we were never as close as my cousins and I were—and they were much closer to each other than they ever were to me. That didn't fully change until I got older and moved away from New York. Now, me and my sister and brother talk daily and see each other as often as we can. We definitely have a better relationship compared to our upbringing, and I'm grateful for the growth we've found together. That distance created space for reflection, healing, and eventually, a better understanding of who we were to each other.*

Those growing pains started to mold me. I began to feel like the black sheep—a child out of place. There were moments where it didn't feel like I belonged anywhere. And while my great-grandmother loved me deeply, I couldn't always see it clearly because of the tension in the home.

My uncles and aunts—and even cousins at times—made me feel like I was too much, or like I had something they didn't. My grandmother spoke up for me and gave me things they didn't have—but I had no control over that. And the way they reacted to it often made me shrink.

I remember my uncle calling me names like "doofus" or "stupid" just for asking questions I genuinely didn't understand. My father's mother—who had taken me from my mom—would call me out of my name like I wasn't even a child. The house was full, but I often felt alone. The only ones who could relate were my younger cousins—but even then, they weren't going through what I was. They were just close enough to witness it. As we've grown, my relationship with them has shifted. One of my cousins and I now speak regularly—every other day or at least once a week—especially as we've both grown closer to the Lord. My relationship with the other cousin is more distant; we fall off sometimes, only speaking around birthdays or family events. We weren't as close as we were growing up, and while that hasn't changed much, it will always be love. No matter what, I've learned to accept my family for who they are while staying true to who I've grown to be.

Still, there was one person who made me feel seen.

My great-grandmother Daisy became my source of comfort, showing me that love can fill gaps in unexpected ways. She made me feel special, always calling me her **"Black Beauty."** Those words filled me with pride and gave me a sense of worth I didn't fully understand until later. I believe she saw something in me that I hadn't even discovered yet—a potential waiting to blossom.

Even with her love, I saw things that shaped my determination to live differently. I witnessed the abuse of alcohol, the heaviness of smoking, the loud cursing, and the heartbreak of cheating. Even as a little girl, I whispered inside, *I don't want this life.*

I didn't know what I wanted to become, but I knew what I didn't. I knew what pain looked like. I knew what silence sounded like. I knew what bitterness tasted like. And I also knew what **resilience** felt like.

I didn't realize it then, but God was protecting my heart. Even in that apartment, even in that family dynamic, even in my confusion—He was planting something deeper in me. Something that would awaken and rise in His timing.

And as you read the chapters ahead, you'll see—God had a way of using every part of it. The rejection. The love. The pain. The promises. It all became part of the transformation. The blueprint. The *becoming.*

One of my favorite ways to escape growing up was playing double dutch. When my friend from upstairs would knock on the door and ask if I could come outside, I knew it was on. That sidewalk was my sanctuary. Jumping rope wasn't just a game—it was my freedom. It was rhythm. It was a place to laugh, to forget, to *breathe*.

And then, there was Yogi Bear. My New Yorkers might know about it—it was a program for kids in the neighborhood where you could dance, sing, play games, and be poured into spiritually. I didn't realize it at the time, but those moments were seeds. Seeds of joy. Seeds of escape. Seeds of God.

Looking back, I see it all clearly now.

The rejection. The abandonment. The misplaced anger. The spiritual confusion. The crowded apartment. The name-calling. The seeds of strength.

I survived it all.

And the truth is—I wasn't just raised. I was *kept*. Covered. Protected. Even when I didn't feel it, God had His hands on me.

My childhood wasn't perfect, but it was **purposeful**. It shaped me, stretched me, and prepared me to become everything I am today. I am not the product of my pain—I'm the product of God's plan.

You don't have to be a product of your environment. You can **take back your birthright** and rise into who God always meant for you to be.

Reflect: What early experience made you stronger even when it hurt?

CHAPTER THREE

Grief and Loss

"You don't get over it—you grow through it."

As I stepped into adulthood, I carried the weight of everything I had seen and survived. I was still trying to understand love, still searching for stability, still holding onto childhood wounds. And then, grief came for me in a way I never saw coming.

At nineteen years old, I experienced the unimaginable—the loss of my first son, Akeeim Jr. On April 5, 2012, I went in for a routine OB-GYN appointment at thirty-five weeks and five days pregnant. I was nervous, but hopeful. I was preparing to be a better mother than what I had experienced. But then, the doctor said the words that shattered me: "There's no heartbeat."

I lost it. Completely. My emotions flooded me, and I feared that my grief might take my mind with it. I remember thinking, *Will I lose myself in this? Will I ever come back from this?* I was the first in my family to go through something like this—and they didn't know how to help me. I felt alone, but God made sure I wasn't.

One of the angels He sent was my nurse, Ms. Vicky. She stayed with me throughout that pregnancy, even through delivery. She gave me her presence when words couldn't fix it. My grandmother stepped in during that devastating time and paid for my son to have a funeral and be cremated. That gesture, that love—it meant everything. Ms. Vicky, if you're reading this—I thank you. I miss you. You were God-sent.

I remember sitting outside one evening, completely consumed by grief. A close friend sat beside me. She didn't try to fix me—she just listened. She shared her own story of loss and reminded me that grief is heavy, but we don't have to carry it alone. Her words stayed with me: *"God makes no mistakes; you will be okay."*

Six weeks later, I found out I was pregnant again—with my son, Zy'mere. He was born on January 19, 2013. When I heard his first cry, it felt like God was breathing life back into me. In that moment, I realized that joy and pain could exist in the same space. Zy'mere was not a replacement—he was redemption. He was light in my darkness.

As life continued, grief didn't stop. At twenty-three, in 2017, I lost two more anchors in my life: my great-grandmother Daisy, and my grandfather—my mother's father. My grandfather was like Malcolm X to the family. He had a commanding voice, wise words, and a presence that grounded you. I wasn't raised by him, but we shared a bond that grew stronger when I was about seventeen. He poured into me, always telling me I was beautiful and capable. I'll never forget his words when I'd ask him how he was doing: *"I'm alive, I'm alive, I'm alive."* He lived a life of strength and no regrets—and I'm proud to be part of his legacy.

After my great-grandmother passed on May 3, 2017, I found out I was pregnant again—with my third son, Marcus Jr. That same year, on my birthday—August 2, 2017—I got engaged. My grandfather passed away on November 20, 2017. Then, I got married on December 14, 2017. Marcus Jr. was born on December 23, 2017. From the moment I held him, I knew he was more than just my son—he was my reminder that God was still writing my story. Marcus brought a sense of peace I didn't know I needed. His birth came at the end of one of the most emotionally overwhelming years of my life, and somehow, his presence grounded me. It was a season filled with joy and pain, celebration and grief. There were days I didn't know whether to smile or scream—grief and celebration felt like they were sitting at the same table. To be honest, so much happened that year, it almost broke me. I walked through death, heartbreak, pregnancy, marriage, and the weight of grief so heavy it nearly crushed me. To know that I survived it all—that I'm still here—is nothing short of a miracle. It's mind-blowing to realize I didn't just make it—I endured what tried to take me out and still kept walking. When my great-grandmother passed, I was angry with God—angry that He took the one person I needed most, the one I depended on. I didn't want to live anymore. I felt empty, lost, and hopeless. But I believe with my whole heart that God placed Marcus Jr. inside of me to keep me. I was ready to end my life, but He gave me a reason to stay.

Now, I understand that God had to take my grandmother so that I would finally learn to depend on Him—not just people. It took years for me to see that. I had to grow into that understanding through the pain, through the silence, and through surrender.

Even with blessings surrounding me, I was still battling brokenness within. In my darkest moments, I allowed grief and confusion to push me into habits that didn't honor who I was becoming. I abused alcohol. I manipulated people. I cheated—not because I didn't care, but because I was trying to heal through people. I was trying to fill a void of grief with lust—confused emotions and unmet needs dressed up in temporary comfort. I hurt people I loved. And yet—God still covered me.

I often asked, *God, how can You still love me after everything I've done?* But His answer was clear: *"My grace is sufficient for you."* I now realize God wasn't punishing me—He was pulling me closer, even when I tried to run. He kept giving me second chances, even when I didn't think I deserved them. He kept loving me, even when I couldn't love myself.

As Maya Angelou once said, *"You may encounter many defeats, but you must not be defeated..."* That quote became my anchor. I've learned that grief doesn't mean the end—it means something new is beginning.

This chapter of my life taught me that grief is not just about losing someone, it's about learning who you are when the pieces fall apart. It's about discovering what still lives inside of you, even after you've buried parts of your heart.

And to anyone reading this who has felt that kind of loss—please hear me: You are not alone. You will rise. You will heal. You will become. Your grief will not break you—it will build you. Over time, I've also had to grieve friendships, and I've learned how to cope with loss in many forms. Grief doesn't always look like death—sometimes it's the letting go of people, places, and seasons.

But in it all, I've discovered that God's grace is steady, and healing continues, layer by layer. And through every loss, every goodbye, every broken piece, I now stand as living proof that grief does not have the final say—**grace does.**

Reflect: What loss in your life revealed the depth of your strength?

_____

_____

_____

_____

_____

_____

_____

CHAPTER FOUR

Relocated (Caterpillar Roams)

"Sometimes God has to move you before He can use you."

Leaving New York on August 15, 2015, with my son Zy'mere was like a breath of fresh air. Sometimes I can't believe I really left after all those years, but I was doing what was necessary for both of us. My cousin was there when we got into the cab from my grandmother's house. Her presence that morning mattered. Over our teenage and adulthood years, we'd grown closer despite our differences, even though we weren't close growing up, and we are still close to this day. It was a quiet reminder from God that even in stepping into the unknown, I wasn't alone.

I was leaving everything I knew to step into a new environment. The plan was for me and Zy'mere's father to meet in Savannah, Georgia, and try to make our relationship and family work. We stayed with Zy'mere's aunt, which felt like a blessing at first—until it wasn't. I'll always be grateful for her support because without it, I couldn't have taken those first steps toward independence and growth.

A week later, Zy'mere's father joined us. The transition from New York to Savannah was rough—the two cities couldn't have been more different. One day, after a small disagreement, I asked Zy'mere's father a question, and he replied, 'Shut up before I slap you.' I replied, 'No, you won't.' You know what happened next? He slapped me. I jumped up to defend myself while my son and his niece and nephew watched. His sister did step in and break it up and told him he had to leave. And he did. However, that moment taught me two truths that have stayed with me: a real man never puts his hands on a woman, and I should never provoke anyone. I was ready to leave and go back to what I knew, but a part of me knew I could survive and needed to stay. I stayed—because it was nothing for me to turn back to.

We had been together since November 2011, and domestic violence had become a pattern I didn't even recognize at the time. I thought it was love. I didn't have a relationship with God yet, and I believed the world owed me something. My grandmother used to say, "You walking around here like the world owe you something." I didn't understand it then, but I do now.

There were moments I wanted to return to New York. One afternoon, while home with Zy'mere, he mimicked his father's behavior—choking me and raising his hand. I had to stop him while crying, realizing how toxic my environment had become. That day, I knew something had to change.

By October, I got my first apartment on my own. I asked my grandmother to watch Zy'mere for a while so I could focus on getting everything together. That apartment represented freedom and independence—a space where I could start building a life for us.

Adjusting to Savannah took time. I made mistakes and met people who didn't have my best interests at heart, but through it all, I learned about my purpose and resilience. In 2020, I hit a low point with my first and only DUI. Driving intoxicated, I could have lost everything. By God's grace, I was stopped before tragedy struck. That moment forced me to face the reality that drinking, a generational curse in my family, controlled me.

I drank after that incident, but on September 27, 2023, God didn't only come into my life and save me—He also helped me fully commit to stop drinking and remove the taste from my mouth. That decision was about stepping fully into my purpose and personal growth. Through the years, I had been stuck in my ways, but after the DUI, I had to learn to evolve and change. I didn't even recognize myself at first, but that experience forced me to confront who I was becoming—and who I was meant to be.

Relocating wasn't just about leaving New York. It was about finally breaking through the shell I had been living in. Like a caterpillar cracking open, I began to evolve, shedding old patterns and stepping into the life I was meant to live. Every roadblock and each learning experience became part of the path that led me to reclaim my power, embrace my growth, and fully step into who I am meant to be.

To the risk-takers, the ones who wonder *"Why Savannah?"*, and anyone stepping into the unknown—this story is proof. It wasn't my plan; it was God's plan. Every risk, every leap into uncertainty, every moment you feel fear—it's part of the journey to the life you're meant to live. Trust it, embrace it, and step boldly. Your growth, your freedom, your purpose—they're waiting on the other side of that leap.

> **Reflect: What part of your story required separation before elevation?**

_____
_____
_____
_____
_____
_____

CHAPTER FIVE

Marriage (Unravled)

"A covenant under God requires more than love—it requires grace."

Happiness doesn't come from simply being with someone; it comes from being your most authentic self with that person, creating unforgettable moments together, and building a partnership where both individuals are free to grow, evolve, and inspire each other every step of the way. But even though I envisioned a certain path for my life, moving to Savannah, facing challenges with my son's dad, and eventually marrying someone new was nowhere near the story I had planned for my future. Yet, sometimes, life has its way of leading us exactly where we need to be.

I met Marcus the same year I moved to Savannah. It may sound unbelievable, but when you are moving so quickly and not taking the time to heal on your own before rushing into something, life will run its course and give you what you asked for. We both ended up working at the same job. Marcus wasn't the type of guy I'd normally seek out, but there was something about him. His approach was smooth, and despite everything I had been through with Zy'mere's father, I wasn't looking for anything serious. But Marcus wasn't just any guy. He was in church, patient, and kind, and showed me a side of life I hadn't realized I was missing and needed.

Our first date was December 11th, 2015—a Friday. We went bowling and then grabbed food and drinks afterward. Something shifted that night. I wasn't just having fun; I was beginning to see a new kind of possibility. Again, I was rushing into something without taking time for myself and my new beginnings. Over time, I noticed how our lives started to blend in beautiful ways—things I loved, he was open to; he was introducing me to new experiences. We were growing together. The next year, we took our first trip together, and that's when I saw Marcus not just as someone I was with, but as the person who showed me how I was meant to be treated. He gave me everything I didn't know I needed and everything I deserved.

We were building something that was beyond just a relationship—it felt like a partnership. Nothing, no challenge, could come between what we were creating. We were both evolving, together in our own ways. In those moments, I realized that love isn't just about finding someone; it's about creating a life with someone—a life that helps you become the person you were always meant to be.

But life, as it often does, has a way of throwing us into the fire to test our strength. In 2017, my world was shaken. My grandmother passed away, and in the same year, I discovered I was pregnant, got engaged in August, and lost my grandfather—all within a few months. It felt as though I was caught in a whirlwind of grief, joy, and transition all at once. Yet, even in the face of such profound loss, I didn't have the luxury to crumble. The only thing I knew was survival—holding it together for the sake of my family, for the sake of my future. I couldn't let myself break, not after everything I had already faced. Grief had to be postponed because the fight for resilience was stronger than the urge to fall apart.

In the midst of it all, I made the decision to get married in December—not just because I wanted to, but because I needed to secure a stable future for my boys. I wasn't willing to take the same risks I had taken before, not after everything that happened with Zy'mere's father. I was in survival mode. I couldn't start a family and risk everything. I also approached our relationship with a level of urgency—talking about marriage, commitment, and next steps—before Marcus was prepared to have those conversations. I gave ultimatums from my experiences and the expectations I had carried into this relationship. And as if the weight of the world wasn't enough, Marcus and I were also advised by our Apostle that we shouldn't have our baby out of wedlock, which heavily influenced our decision to marry. This advice, coupled with the absence of any immediate family around to support us, made it clear that we needed to take control of our situation and build a foundation that was rooted in security, love, and faith.

Then, as if fate was testing us further, Marcus and his dad were in a devastating car accident. I didn't even find out about it until Marcus was back home, safe but shaken. In that moment, I understood something deeply: life doesn't wait for you to be ready. It doesn't stop for you to catch your breath. But strength isn't about how much you can endure—it's about how much you can rise, time and time again, no matter what life throws your way. I realized that resilience isn't just about surviving the storm; it's about learning how to dance in the rain, to find your footing, and keep moving forward even when the road ahead seems uncertain.

After giving birth to Marcus Jr. on December 23rd, 2017, my emotions were a storm, but this time, it felt different. I didn't just feel lost—I felt like I was searching for something deeper, something I couldn't even define. When my 25th birthday came in 2018, I spiraled into a reckless cycle of drinking and smoking, trying to escape the turmoil inside. My decisions led to mistakes, including infidelity, which soon became a pattern I didn't see until I reached my thirties. I had been living defensively for years, overwhelmed with the feeling of not being understood—by others, but most of all, by myself. I thought I was in control, being honest about my actions and mistakes, but deep down, I was still running from my pain, still looking for a way to feel anything different—even if it meant hurting myself.

Growth is not easy, and change can be excruciating, but it is in those moments of discomfort that we encounter the lessons that transform us. These were the lessons that led me to recognize the deep goodness of God, teaching me to surrender to His plan, even when it didn't make sense at the time. There were moments where I found strength and discipline, going months, weeks, and even days without the toxic habits I had been clinging to. But it wasn't until I faced some of my deepest hurts that my perspective began to shift. I was finally ready to understand the power of making hard choices and learning from them.

Then, in 2019, I found out I was pregnant with May'jour and gave birth to him on April 30th, 2020. Fear and uncertainty gripped me at first—I was terrified of the possibility that I had made a mistake, that I had created a life outside of my marriage. But after checking the dates and facing the truth, I realized this child was Marcus' and that we would walk this journey together. In that moment, something shifted. We decided to believe in our future, to trust that we could build something beautiful despite the chaos of our past.

But over time, the connection Marcus and I shared began to shift. Our conversations, affection, and intimacy faded. We both noticed it, but we chose to ignore it, hoping the issues would resolve themselves. We tried to heal together through counseling, prayer, uncomfortable conversations, and working on old patterns, but we couldn't seem to find our way back to the connection we once had. We kept pushing through, but deep down, I knew the truth: I had married Marcus for the wrong reasons. I came into this marriage with trauma, and instead of working on myself, I chose to let him rescue me from my own reality—a reality I still needed to work on with God. I didn't know who I truly was, my worth then, didn't understand my value, and didn't have the standards for myself that I have now.

God doesn't want us to be unhappy, and it wasn't like that in the very beginning. But when there is an awakening inside of you that begins to rise boldly, that's the Holy Spirit giving you strength you lacked on your own, and discernment you did not yet trust. I know the importance of spiritual warfare and praying diligently—for my husband, for myself, and for our family. I understand that interceding prayer, fasting, and obedience are vital, but I also know that a husband must be open to receive help, guidance, and love from his wife. Scripture reminds us, *"Husbands, love your wives, just as Christ loved the church and gave himself up for her"* (Ephesians 5:25). Love, support, and growth are a two-way street—you cannot force someone to do what they are not ready to do.

It's also crucial to set the right example for our children. I am hurt that we have come to this point, but I must continue to trust God and do what He is asking of me. Obedience sometimes comes with hard choices, even when they don't make sense to others. I have to remember that God reminded me, *"Not everyone will understand, and not every conversation with Him is a conference call."* He speaks to us personally, guiding us even when it feels unclear to the world around us. Sometimes that guidance asks us to make choices that others may not understand—like stepping away, standing firm in prayer, or setting boundaries. Listening and responding to Him personally is how we grow in faith, walk in obedience, and set the right example for those around us.

When it comes to marriage, it takes two committed hearts—it takes effort, sacrifice, time, and most importantly, God as the foundation. You can invite Him in, but He must be the firm foundation on which the marriage is built. Looking back, I noticed that over time, Marcus veered away from that foundation, and that's where we were from the beginning. While that was painful, it helped me understand something essential: a marriage can only thrive when both people are committed to growth, faith, and each other.

Today, Marcus and I are no longer together, and we are navigating a divorce. But here's the truth I've learned: life is full of tough decisions. Whether to stay or go, you always have a choice. And no matter how hard the decision may be, you must choose what's best for you. Divorce isn't the end—it's a new beginning. The journey is painful, but it's in that pain that we find our power, our growth, and our purpose. What matters now is how we move forward, as co-parents, as individuals, and as people who have the capacity to grow and evolve. I will forever cherish the moments, lessons, and blessings we've shared. I know now that change is necessary, and with it comes the opportunity to become the best version of ourselves.

Sometimes obedience is not easy—it often requires stepping back, releasing control, and trusting God's perfect timing. Walking away can be a form of surrender, allowing Him to teach, guide, and shape your path. **Obedience to God sometimes means letting go of what we love, so we can embrace what He has for us.** What He produces in the midst of our obedience is often beyond human understanding—something our eyes have never seen and our ears have never heard, yet it is exactly what we were meant to experience.

> **Reflect: What does it look like to release something you love in obedience to God, trusting that His plan is greater than your own?**

_____
_____
_____
_____
_____
_____

CHAPTER SIX

Family/Friends/Community

"Some were seasonal, some were sent, but all were used."

There's something incredibly powerful about the people who enter our lives. The friendships we form, the communities we build, and the relationships we foster all serve as pillars for our transformation. As I reflect on my journey, I am in awe of how these connections have molded me, challenged me, and empowered me to become the woman I am today. And I've come to realize one undeniable truth: the right people in your life aren't just there by chance, they are placed in your path for a reason, to help you discover your strength and to push you toward greatness.

When I moved to Savannah, I embarked on a personal journey of discovery, not just of who I was but of the power of the relationships that would rock with me along the way. Some people came into my life for a season, others who stayed for a reason, and then those who became my pillars—the ones who would remain by my side, unshaken, through all the twists and turns of my growth. Each of them, whether they were with me for a moment or a lifetime, served a critical role in my evolution.

In the years between 2015 and 2022, I was figuring out who I was meant to be. I had always known I had the energy, the spark, the magnetism that drew people in—but I didn't always know who I was. I was on a quest to find my purpose, my worth, and the direction my life was headed. Along the way, I met countless individuals who shaped my journey. Some helped me celebrate, some helped me grow, and others were simply there to give me space to release my emotions when I needed it most.

Through this process, I learned about the kind of friend I am dependable, honest, supportive, a cheerleader, and someone who shares wisdom without being a "yes" friend. I realized that my authenticity and transparency are gifts that guide not only me but those around me. And as I grew closer to God, I was able to build my community—EWWG, Empowering Women With God. Though the idea was given to me on February 5th, 2024, and planted on March 23rd, 2024, I couldn't bring it to life until 2025. I had to trust in God's timing, not my own, which was perfect, and I had to wait for the season to be right.

I discovered that there were three types of people in my life: those who were with me for a season, those who were with me for a reason, and those who would be there for a lifetime. The season people were placed in my life temporarily, sometimes to challenge me, sometimes to teach me lessons, and sometimes to help me overcome specific obstacles. Their presence wasn't permanent, but their impact was profound.

Then, there were the reason people who entered my life at just the right moment, pushing me toward personal growth and awakening something in me I hadn't yet realized. They taught me lessons, offered wisdom, and sparked moments of clarity that propelled me toward the next phase of my transformation.

And lastly, there are the lifetime people. These are the friends, family, and mentors who stay through thick and thin—who believe in you even when you don't believe in yourself, who stand by you when everything else is shifting. These relationships are the foundation of your life, the ones that keep you grounded and encourage you to reach higher, aim further, and dream bigger.

Understanding these roles was a game-changer for me. It allowed me to release the need to have everyone in my life forever and instead focus on nurturing the connections that truly mattered. I stopped seeking validation from the wrong places and started to recognize the value of relationships aligned with my purpose. I realized I was never truly alone—I had a powerful network of friends, family, and mentors who had always been there, even when I hadn't recognized their presence.

As I grew through each season, I began to understand that life is a journey of transformation and metamorphosis, much like the butterfly. When we start, we are like the caterpillar, born with potential, growing, adapting, and finding our way. But there comes a time when we have to break free of the old, shed the past, and embrace the discomfort that change brings. The caterpillar must go through a complete transformation before it can emerge as a butterfly, and so do we.

Change is never easy. It challenges us, forces us to confront our deepest fears, and asks us to let go of what no longer serves us. But as we evolve, we emerge stronger, wiser, and more aligned with who we are truly meant to be. This process of change is exactly how we unlock the fullest version of ourselves. It is through these trials that we find our wings and learn to soar.

Looking back, I realized I was never truly lost. I was in the process of becoming. The relationships that have been part of my journey, all served to guide me through the process of becoming who I am today. They gave me strength when I wanted to give up, reminding me of my worth when I forgot, and helped me realize that transformation isn't something to fear, it's something to embrace.

And now, as I stand in the fullness of my transformation, I am amazed at the woman I am today. The road was not always easy, but it was worth every step. I've learned that the most powerful thing you can do is surround yourself with the right people who uplift you, challenge you, and encourage you to be your best self. The community you build becomes the foundation of your strength and the fuel for your growth.

So, to everyone reading this, I want to remind you: You are not meant to do this alone. The family, friends, and community you cultivate are not just part of the journey—they are the force that drives you toward greatness. Cherish those who walk beside you. Let go of those who no longer align with your growth. And trust that with every relationship, whether fleeting or lasting, you are becoming the person you were always meant to be.

Embrace the transformation. Own your power. And know that the best is yet to come.

Reflect: Who in your life shaped your growth—even if they couldn't stay?

_____
_____
_____
_____
_____
_____
_____
_____
_____
_____

CHAPTER SEVEN

Cocoon (Transformation Begins)

"The cocoon is dark, but it's where wings are formed."

There comes a pivotal moment in life when you can no longer deny the truth about who you've become and what needs to change. For me, that moment came on September 27th, 2023, when God saved me and I fully surrendered my life to Him. I had spent years believing I was untouchable, convinced I had everything figured out—that I could handle anything. But life has a way of humbling us, shaking us to our core, and showing us exactly how much we've been holding on to a false sense of control.

It took real pain and heartache for me to face myself—admitting things I wasn't ready to see. I had hurt people in ways I never thought would come back to me, and yet, here I was, confronted by the same pain I once caused. When I was betrayed by someone I deeply loved and trusted, I had no choice but to face the truth: I had lost my grip. I had lost control, and it was time to regain what I had let slip away.

The heartbreak was unbearable, but it was also the moment I had to decide: Would I stay stuck in hurt and anger, or would I rise above it and transform into something greater? I remember reaching out to the mother of the person who had hurt me, desperate for answers. She said, "The more you think about reaching out to my child, the Lord is standing at the door of your heart, waiting to answer."

At first, I resisted. My flesh wanted to react and fix things on my own terms. But God was inviting me to surrender—to let go of my need for control and allow His healing to take root. That was my cocoon moment. The old version of me, who thought she could handle everything alone, had to die so the new, empowered version could emerge. The cocoon is a hard stage to avoid when God chose you. Answering His call means stepping into a season of growth, challenge, and discomfort—but it is precisely in that challenge where we find the strength to rise.

Once I gave my life over to the Lord, I realized life wasn't going to be easier, but it would be better. I gained knowledge and wisdom, learning that my life was not my own. God used my suffering and endurance to prepare me to minister, guide, and help others. Through this process, I found support, guidance, and accountability in my church—First Tabernacle Missionary Baptist Church—where I was reborn and baptized on March 6, 2024. My church community became a living example of God's love, reinforcing that transformation, while hard, is always purposeful and guided by Him.

From the moment I surrendered on September 27th, my life began to change in ways I couldn't have imagined. God guided me through simple yet profound acts of devotion—walking daily, worshiping, studying His Word, and reflecting in solitude. These practices transformed me from the inside out and helped me embrace the new habits and mindset necessary for my growth.

As I reflect on my journey, I am reminded of God's Word: *"Before I formed you in the womb I knew you; before you were born I set you apart, I appointed you as a prophet to the nations."* (Jeremiah 1:5) Even before my life began, God had a plan, and He knew every trial I would face, every lesson I would learn, and every person He would equip me to help. My surrender and growth were never random—they were part of God's divine design.

God showed me that I had to be willing to transition into what lay ahead to be transformed. Which is a journey, not a one-time event. Life will bring valleys, but it's in those valleys that we grow. The strength we gain carries us to higher ground. Every challenge, every uncomfortable moment, is part of the process. Nothing is wasted, and God uses it all to mold, reshape, and prepare us for something greater.

Looking back, I see how far I've come. Who could have imagined that at the age of thirty I'd be standing strong in faith, boldly witnessing God's glory? I went from barely understanding what it meant to know Him to becoming a living example of His love and guidance.

To you, the reader: The road to transformation isn't easy. You might face doubts, challenges, or moments of uncertainty. But nothing is too difficult for God. Step into the unknown, surrender what holds you back, and trust His timing. There's a butterfly waiting to emerge from your cocoon, and it is ready to take flight. Your best days are ahead of you.

Reflect: What part of you had to break in order for your healing to begin?

_____
_____
_____
_____
_____
_____
_____

CHAPTER EIGHT

Lessons Learned

"The pain didn't break you—it built you."

Life is not a destination—it's an ongoing journey, filled with growth, discovery, and constant transformation. Every moment, every experience, and every encounter carries with it a lesson—some are gentle whispers while others come as powerful revelations that shake us to our core. If you've been living this thing called life, you've likely faced moments that challenged you, changed you, and ultimately shaped you into the person you are today. The truth is, we are never truly done learning. It's the lessons, both big and small, that empower us to evolve and rise higher than before. Embrace them, because each lesson holds the key to unlocking a stronger, wiser, and more empowered version of yourself.

Many of the lessons I've learned didn't fully reveal themselves until I changed my perspective and allowed myself to experience things I had once been afraid of. There were times when I ignored the subtle whispers of wisdom, choosing to hold on to old habits and patterns. Some lessons came to me repeatedly because I refused to learn from them at first. One of the most powerful lessons was the importance of treating others with love and kindness. It wasn't until I faced the truth about myself, after being confronted about my attitude and the way I believed the world revolved around me, that I began to see how deeply I needed to change. I realized that I didn't know how to properly handle my emotions and feelings. But through this realization, I found the strength to seek healing. Speaking openly with a therapist, surrendering my pain to God, journaling my thoughts, and confiding in trusted friends became the tools that helped me shift. In the process, I learned that true power lies in vulnerability, self-reflection, and the willingness to grow.

As I learned the importance of treating others with kindness and love, I realized the next crucial step was to turn that same compassion inward. Another lesson I had to learn was how to give myself permission to love myself before I could truly love others. To do this, I needed to spend more intentional alone time with myself—time to be patient and allow myself to understand that love isn't just about material things or outward gestures. It's about nurturing qualities like gentleness, compassion, and affection. As I focused on cultivating these qualities, I began to experience joyful, intentional moments that allowed me to feel, discover, and embrace the changes happening within me. I started to see how this process was unlocking a kind of love I had never fully experienced for myself. God's presence in my life became more tangible during this journey, as I felt Him speaking softly to my heart, teaching me that the love I was seeking had always been within me because He loved me first.

In that journey, I learned the importance of validating myself, of giving myself what I needed to take the next step in my growth—whether it was for me or for anyone who encountered me. I began to realize that self-love wasn't just a luxury, it was a necessity. I came to understand that in order to impact others, I had to first cultivate love within myself. As the Bible says, "Love your neighbor as you love yourself." My interpretation of this scripture became clear: I had to learn to love myself before I could truly love and care for others.

I began to see myself the way God sees me—as precious, worthy, and loved. This shift in perspective empowered me to start complimenting myself in the mirror, repeating affirmations that affirmed my worth, and speaking life into my own soul. I treated myself to experiences that brought me joy, whether I was alone or with others. I wrote letters to my future self and challenged myself with self-love exercises to discover what resonated with me. Every step of the way, I was building a love that reflected who I was on the inside—a love that became the foundation of everything I did. As I always say, "Self-love is a reflection of who you are internally, and it radiates outward, shaping the way you engage with the world." Through this process, I realized that the more I loved myself, the more I was able to share that love with the world.

There are so many lessons over my thirty-plus years of living that I could share, but the one that resonates most is the power of perspective and perception. How we view the world around us—our relationships, our opportunities, our challenges—can profoundly impact the decisions we make. This lesson became clear to me as I reflected on my own life and recognized the significant role my family, community, and partnerships have played in shaping me. It wasn't always easy to navigate, but the journey of understanding how these influences shaped my choices taught me that perspective truly is everything.

One of the most pivotal lessons I learned was realizing how deeply I had resisted being like anyone in my family. I was determined to carve my own path, one that didn't just reflect the expectations of others but also aligned with my purpose. The desire to make a positive impact in the world—to be a light in others' lives—became my guiding force. But I also understood that this would not come without a commitment to myself. If I truly wanted to be the change I sought, I first had to embrace accountability, honesty, and transparency with myself. These core values became my foundation, and I knew that in order to live the life I envisioned, I had to take ownership of my journey.

I knew what I wanted, but the question remained: How was I going to get there? The answer wasn't an easy one, but it became clear that it all came down to the tools I had accumulated over the years—tools like discipline, consistency, sacrifice, and patience. These pillars of growth had become second nature to me, woven into my daily life. Every challenge I faced, every season I walked through, was an opportunity to refine these tools and put them into practice. I understood that life would not always unfold the way I wanted, but I knew I had the power to pivot, adjust, and move forward.

Discipline gave me the structure to keep moving even when motivation waned. Consistency kept me grounded, helping me to show up for myself and for others, day in and day out. Sacrifice taught me the importance of letting go of what didn't serve me so I could make room for what truly mattered. And patience—oh, how patience helped me grow through the moments of uncertainty, teaching me to trust the process and allow things to unfold in divine timing.

But what really kept me going, what really kept me grounded in the midst of it all, was my purpose. My gift—the one that always found its way to the surface even in the most challenging times—was constantly showing up. It was my beacon of light, guiding me through the darkness, reminding me of why I had started in the first place. My purpose has always been my anchor, my source of strength, and the reminder that everything I experienced was a stepping stone to becoming the person I was meant to be.

As I look back on my journey, I see how all these lessons have converged to create a life filled with meaning and purpose. Each lesson, each challenge, each triumph was part of a bigger plan that was far beyond anything I could have imagined. And while my journey is far from over, I now understand that the power to create the life I desire lies within me. I have everything I need to continue moving forward with confidence and clarity, knowing that each step is part of a beautiful unfolding.

"The journey to becoming the best version of yourself is not defined by the destination but by the strength you gain from every lesson, the wisdom you uncover from every challenge, and the resilience you build from every trial. You are not just a product of your past but a masterpiece in the making, created for purpose and greatness."

Reflect: What lesson have you finally stopped resisting?

CHAPTER NINE

Butterfly (Takeoff)

"You're not becoming her—you already are her."

As I reflect on my journey, it's clear: I've already taken off. I've felt the wind beneath my wings and soared higher with each step I've taken. This chapter isn't about waiting for my flight to begin—it's about recognizing that I've been soaring for quite some time now. The path I've walked—marked by challenges, triumphs, and transformation—has prepared me for this very moment. And as I write these words today, I know deep within my spirit: I'm only just beginning to touch the heights I'm destined to achieve.

Gratitude has been my foundation. It has been the steady rhythm behind every stride, fueling my momentum and carrying me forward through every season of my life. With discipline, willingness, and unshakable faith as my guiding principles, I have conquered obstacles that once felt immovable. I've risen above setbacks that tried to break me, and I've reached heights I once believed were out of reach. These moments weren't just lessons; they became the winds that lifted me higher and higher, empowering me to soar.

My name is Ernaysia Woods, and it is my God-given purpose to help other women take flight—just as I have. But my journey didn't begin with some sudden, grand transformation. It began with embracing each stage life required of me. From the egg, to the caterpillar, to the cocoon, every stage was necessary. Every phase—no matter how uncomfortable or uncertain—was shaping and refining me into the woman I am today. And now, as a butterfly, I don't just fly—I soar with confidence, direction, and divine purpose.

Through every challenge, I chose to trust the process. I stopped leaning on my own understanding and began leaning into the divine guidance that had always been waiting for me. God's plan for my life has always been bigger than anything I could have written for myself, and the more I surrendered to His will, the more I grew in grace, wisdom, and strength.

Today, I am living proof of His faithfulness. I've accomplished more than I once thought possible through *Elevate Your Destiny LLC*—a vision born from my passion for growth, healing, and transformation. Through personal growth coaching, I've walked beside women as they've broken free from limitations and stepped boldly into their next chapter. As a public speaker and host, I've shared stages and shared my story, not just to inspire, but to empower others to rise above their own battles.

Throughout my transformative sessions, which are called "Tap Into You". During these events, I've witnessed women light up as they rediscover their beauty, their power, and their worth, seeing not just who they are, but who they were always meant to be. Because transformation isn't just internal—it radiates outward, and when a woman feels aligned with her true self, the world sees her differently.

But I know this: none of it would have been possible without God. Every door that opened, every breakthrough, every opportunity was orchestrated by Him. I am standing here as living proof that with God, all things are possible.

When I look back, I see clearly—I didn't get here on my own. It was His strength that carried me. It was His voice that guided me. It was His grace that lifted me when I didn't think I could rise again. And now, I stand here, not just as a woman who has soared, but as a woman determined to show you that you can soar too.

You have already begun your flight, whether you see it or not. The challenges you've faced, the storms you've weathered, the lessons you've endured—those weren't setbacks. They were training grounds, preparing you for the wings you already carry. Now it's your time to spread them fully. There is no hurdle too high, no mountain too steep, no challenge too great. The dreams you've been holding in your heart aren't too big—they're Waiting for you to answer.

Transformation is not a one-time event; it is a continuous journey. It requires faith when the path looks uncertain, discipline when it feels easier to quit, and a willingness to grow when growth feels uncomfortable. But if you trust the process, you will rise—not just into the ordinary, but into the extraordinary.

The sky is waiting, and you are more than ready.

And together, we will continue to rise. Together, we will soar beyond what we ever thought possible. And as we look back one day, full of gratitude for every stage of the journey, we will know without a doubt: with God's guidance, there is no ceiling to our flight. The sky is not the limit—it's only the beginning of what God has in store.

> **Reflect: What's one truth about yourself you're ready to embrace—fully and fearlessly?**

_____
_____
_____
_____
_____
_____

AS I FLY
By: Ernaysia Woods

In the cradle of dawn, I stretch my wings wide,
Emerging from shadows where doubts used to hide.
With each gentle breeze, I dance and I soar,
Embracing my journey, I'm destined for more.

Through valleys of struggle, I learned how to stand,
With faith as my compass and love at my hand.
The weight of my past I release and let go,
For the sky is my canvas, my spirit will glow.

With dreams as my guide, I chase the unknown,
Each challenge I meet, in resilience I've grown.
No longer confined by the fears that I knew,
I fly with a purpose, my heart beating true.

Each moment a blessing, each breath a new start,
In the strength of my journey, I share from the heart.
As I soar toward the sun, my soul takes flight,
A testament of change, in the brilliance of my light.

In honor and memory of my cousin "TJ"—FLY HIGH, 11/11/2024

THE TRANSFORMATIVE 5: DAILY STEPS TO A BETTER YOU

Tip 1: Practice Daily Gratitude

Start each day by reflecting on three things you're grateful for. For example, I'm grateful for life, my family, and the strength to keep going. Gratitude shifts your focus from what's lacking to what you have, fostering a positive mindset and resilience.

Tip 2: Set Intentions

Before diving into your daily tasks, set intentions for how you want to show up. Whether it's being present in conversations or tackling challenges with determination, setting intentions directs your energy toward meaningful actions.

Tip 3: Spend Time with God

Create a sacred space for prayer, meditation, or reading the word. Spending time with God grounds you in faith, offering guidance, strength, and perspective as you navigate daily challenges.

Tip 4: Embrace Self-Reflection

Take time at the end of each day to journal or meditate on your experiences. Self-reflection allows you to identify patterns, celebrate successes, and learn from challenges, empowering you to grow continuously.

Tip 5: Surrender and Trust

Release worries and anxieties through surrendering to God's plan. Trust that His wisdom and love will guide your path, allowing you to approach each day with peace and confidence in His purpose for your life.

TEN POWERFUL, TRANSFORMATIVE SCRIPTURES

1. **Romans 5:8:** But God demonstrates his own love for us in this: While we were still sinners, Christ died for us.
2. **Hebrews 12:11:** No discipline seems pleasant at the time, but painful. Later on, however, it produces a harvest of righteousness and peace for those who have been trained by it.
3. **Matthew 11:28:** Come to me, all you who are weary and burdened, and I will give you rest.
4. **Psalms 139:1:** You have searched me, Lord, and you know me.
5. **Exodus 33:17:** And the Lord said to Moses, "I will do the very thing you have asked, because I am pleased with you and I know you by name."
6. **Jeremiah 1:5:** Before I formed you in the womb I knew you, before you were born I set you apart; I appointed you as a prophet of the nations.
7. **Romans 8:2:** Because through Christ Jesus the law of the spirit who gives life has set you free from the law of sin and death.
8. **Philippians 4:6:** Do not be anxious about anything, but in every situation, by prayer and petition, with thanksgiving, present your requests to God.
9. **Romans 12:2:** Do not conform to the patterns of this world, but be transformed by the renewing of your mind. Then you will be able to test and approve what God's will is his good, pleasing and perfect will.
10. **Proverbs 3:5-6:** Trust in the lord with all your heart and lean not on your own understanding; in all your ways submit to him and he will make your paths straight.

ABOUT THE AUTHOR

**Hey, I'm Ernaysia Woods
—and it's not just my name, I'm a movement.**

I'm a woman who's been broken, built, and beautifully transformed. Everything I write, speak, and create comes from a real place—because I've lived it. My journey hasn't been perfect, but it's been purposeful. And now I get to help others walk through their own transformation.

I was born in **Brooklyn, New York**, where I went through the first two stages of my becoming: **awareness** and **acceptance**. That's where I survived. That's where I started waking up to who I was, what I was carrying, and what I no longer wanted to stay stuck in.

But it was in **Savannah, Georgia** where everything shifted. That's where I stepped into **willingness** and **discipline**—where I stopped just existing and started becoming. Becoming the woman I needed. The mother my three kings deserve. The vessel God created me to be.

I wear many titles: **Speaker. Host. Coach. Author. God's vessel.**

But at the core of it all, my purpose is rooted in one thing— **reminding people of who they really are.**

Because I know what it feels like to forget.
To shrink.
To give so much of yourself that you lose your reflection.
I've been there. And now, I help others rise from that place.

That's why I created **Elevate Your Destiny**—not just as a brand, but as a **movement**.

A voice for the people.
A space for the overlooked, the healing, and the ready-to-rise.
It's for those tired of pretending they're okay when they're craving transformation.
It's for the ones who are ready to grow through what they go through.

Many people know me as "the host with the most energy"—because when I show up, I don't just bring a mic, I bring a message. I bring truth, power, and presence. Whether I'm speaking on a stage, hosting an event, coaching a client through a breakthrough, or sitting in *The Orange Room*—I show up fully, faithfully, and unapologetically.

I believe:
Pain isn't your identity—it's your invitation.
Healing is holy.
You don't need a platform to be powerful—you just need to be real.
And transformation always starts in the dark—before the glow-up.

Before the Transformation isn't just a book—it's my heart in written form.
It's for the woman who's been silently struggling, holding it all together, and praying for a sign that it's her time.

Sis, this is your sign.
This is your invitation.
You can heal. You can rise. You can become.

If you're ready to start your journey, Want to book me to speak, coach, or host? Let's connect:
👉 www.elevateyourdestiny.com

Let's grow. Let's shift. Let's elevate—together.

REFLECTIVE WRITING
This space is yours.

You've read my truth—now it's time to write yours.
Use the following pages to reflect, release, and reconnect.
Transformation starts when you pause long enough to listen.

| **What part of my story do you see yourself in?**

What transformation do you feel God is calling you into?

What have you outgrown that it's time to release?

What does your "butterfly" season look like?

What do you need to forgive yourself for?

www.ingramcontent.com/pod-product-compliance
Lightning Source LLC
Chambersburg PA
CBHW030447100526
44580CB00001B/20